# TOTAL GYMNASTICS

BY BLYTHE LAWRENCE

SportsZone

An Imprint of Abdo Publishing
www.abdopublishing.com

**abdopublishing.com**

Published by Abdo Publishing, a division of ABDO, PO Box 398166, Minneapolis, Minnesota 55439. Copyright © 2017 by Abdo Consulting Group, Inc. International copyrights reserved in all countries. No part of this book may be reproduced in any form without written permission from the publisher. SportsZone™ is a trademark and logo of Abdo Publishing.

Printed in the United States of America, North Mankato, Minnesota
102016
012017

Cover Photos: Amy Sanderson/Cal Sport Media/AP Images, foreground; Tom Kuest/Fotograf/Shutterstock Images, background
Interior Photos: Tom Kuest/Fotograf/Shutterstock Images, 1; Jeff Roberson/AP Images, 4–5; Brendan Howard/Shutterstock Images, 6; Shutterstock Images, 8–9; Louisa Gouliamaki/AFP/Getty Images, 10; AP Images, 13, 16, 29; URN:4208147/Press Association/AP Images, 14–15; Sasha Samardzija/Shutterstock Images, 18–19; Lilyana Vynogradova/Shutterstock Images, 20; Grace Chiu/UPI/Newscom, 23; Laura Stone/Shutterstock Images, 24; Paul Vathis/AP Images, 26–27; Gregory Bull/AP Images, 30–31, 50–51; Tony Gutierrez/AP Images, 32; Yves Logghe/AP Images, 35; Rob Carr/AP Images, 36–37; Kyodo/AP Images, 39, 40–41; Elise Amendola/AP Images, 42; Rebecca Blackwell/AP Images, 45, 46–47, 53; Gerald Herbert/AP Images, 48; Julio Cortez/AP Images, 54–55; Amy Sanchetta/AP Images, 56; Paulus Ponizak/AP Images, 59; Mikko Stig/Rex Features/AP Images, 60

Editor: Patrick Donnelly
Series Designer: Jake Nordby

**Publisher's Cataloging-in-Publication Data**

Names: Lawrence, Blythe, author.
Title: Total gymnastics / by Blythe Lawrence.
Description: Minneapolis, MN : Abdo Publishing, 2017. | Series: Total sports |
    Includes bibliographical references and index.
Identifiers: LCCN 2016945672 | ISBN 9781680785043 (lib. bdg.) | ISBN
    9781680798326 (ebook)
Subjects:  LCSH: Gymnastics--Juvenile literature.
Classification: DDC 796.44--dc23
LC record available at http://lccn.loc.gov/2016945672

# CONTENTS

# GET TO KNOW
# GYMNASTICS

**B**ang . . . bang . . . bang!

The sound echoes throughout the arena. It is the sound of hands and feet hitting wood and leather. Simone Biles is tumbling on the balance beam. It's another of her breathtaking passes. She's spinning down a 4-inch (10-cm) plank 4 feet (1.2 m) above the ground. But the world's top gymnast doesn't hesitate for a millisecond.

As her feet hit the edge of the beam, Biles launches herself skyward. She appears to take flight. She does two backflips with a full twist.

Simone Biles is famous for her brilliant routines on the balance beam.

Judges closely watch a gymnast's every move.

Then she lands gracefully on the ground. The crowd showers
her with applause.

Biles has everything needed to be successful in
gymnastics. She's quick, strong, and flexible. Most of all, she
loves what she does.

Gymnastics combines performance art and intense athletic competition. No two routines are the same in gymnastics. Champions are determined by a panel of judges. The judges score routines based on the difficulty of the skills gymnasts perform. They also look at execution, or how well each skill is done. Artistry is important, too.

Gymnastics has been around for more than 2,000 years. It is one of the most popular sports at the Olympic Games. Today, approximately 5 million children in the United States practice gymnastics. Fans enjoy watching top-level competitions such as the World Championships and the Olympics. They want to see the best athletes compete for glory and gold medals.

## SIX TYPES

**Artistic gymnastics is the most popular form of the sport. It dominates the airwaves during the summer Olympics. But there are five other types of gymnastics. They are rhythmic, trampoline, acrobatic, aerobic, and Gymnastics for All.**

There's much more to gymnastics than what we see in the Olympics. But that's really where gymnastics got its start.

# 2 GREEK ROOTS

**A**ncient Greeks would probably not recognize their sport today. Still, the roots of modern gymnastics are unmistakably Greek. Gymnastics was born in Greece more than 2,000 years ago. Physical fitness was important to the ancient Greeks. Their culture valued warriors and athletes.

The Greeks devoted a lot of time to athletic feats such as running, tumbling, and vaulting. They trained in gymnasiums to make their bodies strong. In the beginning, "gymnastics" meant all the activities practiced in the gymnasium.

The first modern Olympics were held at the Panathenaic Stadium in Athens, Greece.

Olive wreaths were made from branches cut from trees that grew near the Temple of Zeus in Olympia.

These activities were fun. They also prepared men for physical trials they might face later in life.

As far back as 3,000 years ago, a festival was held in the Greek city of Olympia. Today we know this sporting festival as the Olympic Games. The best athletes from all over Greece participated. They traveled to Olympia every four years for the Games.

The prize for winning an Olympic event wasn't a gold medal. Champions donned an olive wreath, or *kotinos*. But Olympic heroes earned something even better. To be an Olympic champion meant eternal fame. Your name would live on forever.

The ancient Olympic Games took place for more than 1,000 years. But in the year 393 CE, the Roman Emperor Theodosius I stopped the Olympic Games. It would be another 1,500 years before the world heard of them again.

Greece wasn't the only place where gymnastics exercises flourished. Moves such as handstands and backflips were practiced from the Middle East to Asia in ancient times.

Germany won five of the eight gold medals in gymnastics at the first modern Olympic Games.

Europe's traveling acrobats thrilled audiences with their juggling and dancing. Soldiers also did gymnastic exercises as part of their training.

In the 1700s, exercising became a popular trend in central Europe. Physical education professors found new ways to build muscles. A German professor named Fredrich Ludwig Jahn developed gymnastics equipment. He invented the balance beam and parallel bars.

Sports clubs also became popular over time. People went to clubs to practice these new activities. Most importantly the Olympic Games returned. The first modern Olympics were held in Athens, Greece, in 1896. Gymnastics was one of nine sports contested that year. The gymnasts, all of them male,

## NAKED SPORT

The word "gymnasium" comes from the Greek word *gymnos*, meaning "naked." Athletes in ancient Greece wore very little clothing as they practiced sports. Gymnastics as we know it today was not a sport at the ancient Olympic Games. However, it was a big part of Greek life.

Carl Schuhmann of Germany won the gold medal on the men's horse vault at the 1896 Athens Games.

competed in events such as parallel bars, pommel horse, and the rope climb. A new era had begun.

# 3

# WOMEN TAKE THE STAGE

**A**fter the 1896 Olympic Games, men's gymnastics gained popularity as a sport. Europeans flocked to join gymnastics clubs. The sport also spread to the United States and South America. German immigrants introduced the basic concepts of the sport. They also founded gymnastics clubs in numerous cities.

The Olympic movement grew, too. The events that were included in gymnastics competitions varied by location. For example, pole vaulting was a gymnastics event at the 1900 Paris Games.

Women performed gymnastics routines at the 1908 London Olympics, but they were not allowed to compete for another 20 years.

Despite its growing popularity, only half the population was allowed to participate. As in ancient Greece, women were forbidden to compete in gymnastics at the Olympic Games. But soon women asserted their right to participate.

The roots of women's gymnastics lie in physical fitness. Dance and rhythmic movements played a big role in the development of the sport. Women's gymnastics made its Olympic debut in 1928 in Amsterdam, the Netherlands. Teams performed group exercises in unison, with no equipment. But it wouldn't stay that way for long.

## ITALY'S SILVER STAR

Carla Marangoni had a big year in 1928. She celebrated her 13th birthday. And with her Italian teammates she won an Olympic silver medal in women's gymnastics. Exercises were held outdoors in the Olympic stadium that year. And there were no mats. Marangoni celebrated her 100th birthday in November 2015.

Cissy Davies of Great Britain competes on the balance beam at the 1948 Summer Olympics in London, England.

# 4

# AROUND THE GYM

By the early 1950s, the sport of gymnastics began to look more like it does today. At the 1952 Olympics in Helsinki, Finland, women began competing in four events. Those events are the same that are used in today's Olympics: vault, uneven bars, balance beam, and floor exercise. The men had six events: floor exercise, pommel horse, still rings, vault, parallel bars, and high bar.

## VAULT

Vaulting is the closest gymnasts come to flying. They sprint down a narrow runway toward the vaulting table. Then they hit a springboard and

A young gymnast performs on the vault.

bounce toward the table. After pushing off the table with their hands, they rocket through the air. They perform flips or twists before landing. The best gymnasts go both high and far, landing a great distance from the table.

## UNEVEN BARS

Swinging well is the key to success on the uneven parallel bars. Gymnasts swing from bar to bar. A gymnast isn't allowed to slow down or stop her routine on the uneven bars. She also has to make sure her feet never touch the ground during her exercise.

Women perform to music during the floor exercise, but men do not.

## BALANCE BEAM

The long, narrow balance beam is 4 feet (1.2 m) high and 16 feet (4.9 m) long. It's just 4 inches (10 cm) wide. The best gymnasts make the leaps and flips on the beam look easy.

The uneven bars are a true test of strength, agility, and concentration.

## SPRING TRAINING

**Many gyms have springy trampolines along with traditional gymnastics equipment. The trampoline is a gymnastics discipline in its own right. But it's also an excellent place to learn and practice new skills for floor exercise or vault. Plus it's just fun to bounce on it!**

But one false move can cause a gymnast to fall to the ground. It takes a lot of hard work to master the beam.

## FLOOR EXERCISE

Floor exercise routines contain many different elements. They combine leaps, jumps, turns, and dance. But the highlights are the spectacular tumbling passes of flips and twists. Gymnasts begin a tumbling pass in one corner of the floor. They crisscross the mat diagonally, arriving in the other corner. Competition floors have springs under the mats, allowing gymnasts to fly higher. Floor exercise is the event that allows the most creativity and personal expression. As a result, floor is a favorite of many gymnasts.

The iron cross is an important position in a still rings routine.

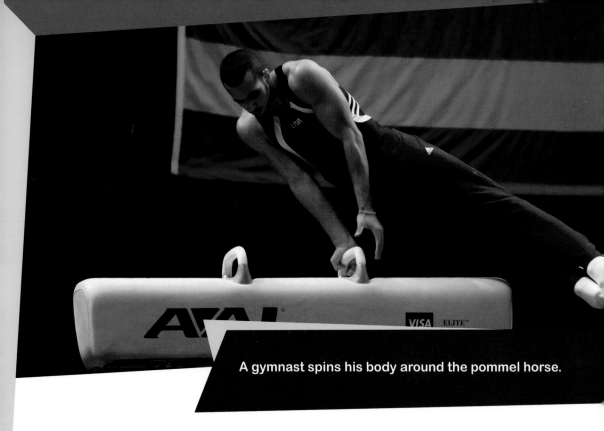

A gymnast spins his body around the pommel horse.

## STILL RINGS

The still rings are the ultimate test of force. Male gymnasts hang from the rings and contort themselves into strength positions such as the famous iron cross. A gymnast who is good on still rings is usually easy to spot. Look for the guy with the biggest biceps on the team.

## POMMEL HORSE

The pommel horse is like the balance beam, but for hands instead of feet. Only men perform on it. Gymnasts rotate their bodies in circles around the leather-covered horse. Often only their hands are touching the horse and its two handles.

## PARALLEL BARS

The parallel bars test a male gymnast's coordination and flexibility. The gymnast relies on his hands and arms during this exercise. The best gymnasts do midair flips and catch the bars with their upper arms.

**Both men and women perform floor exercises on a square mat 40 feet (12.2 m) per side.**

## HIGH BAR

High bar is an event for daredevils. The bar stands 10 feet (3 m) above the ground. Male gymnasts swing around the bar in big circles called giants. They also do release moves, which delight fans at competitions. To do a release move, the gymnast lets go of the bar. He then flies through the air, does a flip or a twist, and catches the bar again without touching the ground.

# 5

# PERFECTION

Nadia Comăneci was not thinking about perfection. It was the first day of the gymnastics competition at the 1976 Olympic Games in Montreal, Quebec, Canada. As the 14-year-old from Romania mounted the uneven bars to begin her routine, she was just hoping to do a good exercise.

But fate had something else in store for the slight, brown-haired teen. After Nadia landed her dismount and saluted to the judges, a strange thing happened. The scoreboard flashed her score as 1.00.

Nadia Comăneci dismounts from the uneven bars after the first perfect routine in Olympic history.

Nadia and her teammates were puzzled. Nadia's routine had been excellent. Certainly the low score was a mistake?

## MR. PERFECT

**The first man to score a perfect 10 in Olympic competition was Alexander Dityatin. He was the star of the 1980 Olympics in his home country, the Soviet Union. Dityatin scored a 10 on vault. He also won a medal in every individual event. Dityatin racked up eight medals at the Moscow Games. No athlete has ever won more medals at one Olympic Games.**

Suddenly a big cheer rose from the crowd. They realized the judges had given Nadia a perfect score. It had never happened at the Olympics. Perfection was unheard of. It hadn't even been considered. The scoreboard was not designed to show a score higher than 9.99. Instead, it had shown 1.00.

Nadia's perfect 10 made her famous. She went on to record six more perfect 10s at the Montreal Games. Other gymnasts have since followed with perfect performances at the Olympic Games. Still, Nadia's are remembered as some of the most special moments in gymnastics history.

That's not 1.0—that's a perfect 10 on the scoreboard behind Nadia Comăneci at the 1976 Summer Games in Montreal.

Nadia's performance at the 1976 Olympics was a turning point in the sport. She represented a totally new kind of gymnastics. Nadia was younger and lighter than gymnasts of the past. She could do jaw-dropping acrobatic skills. Nobody had ever seen anything like her routines. Gymnasts around the world rushed to copy Nadia's style. They mastered even harder skills.

Gymnastics would never be the same.

# 6

# JUDGING CHANGES

McKayla Maroney glided down the vaulting runway at the 2012 Olympic Games in London, England. She focused on the vault she was about to perform. The team gold medal was on the line.

McKayla's vault was one of the most difficult skills in all of gymnastics. It included a flip with two and a half twists. McKayla was one of the best vaulters in the world. She wanted to show the judges how well she could do.

Her feet hit the springboard and her body soared high into the air. She got enough height

McKayla Maroney sticks the landing during the team competition of the 2012 Olympic Games.

Judges keep a close eye on a vaulter.

to complete her twists. Then she stuck the landing. McKayla threw her arms in the air. Her vault had been nearly perfect.

In the past, McKayla's vault might have received a score of 10. For a long time, the best score a gymnast could earn was a perfect 10. But 10 is no longer the ultimate score in gymnastics. A new scoring system was adopted in 2006.

A gymnast's score is now determined by two factors. One factor is the difficulty of skills involved in the routine. That score is often referred to as the "degree of difficulty." The other scoring factor is the execution of the routine. That means how well it was performed. Execution judges start at 10 and deduct points when they see faults. On the international level, the difficulty score is added to the execution score. That creates one total score.

Gymnastics scoring today is different from the system that gave Nadia Comăneci her

## BASIC DEDUCTIONS

**Nobody's perfect. Still, gymnasts strive for the very best. A gymnast's routine is always evaluated by judges. They carefully watch the routines, looking for small mistakes. For every error, judges deduct points. Deductions tend to be small for minor errors, such as a slight wobble on the balance beam. A gymnast who slips off an apparatus or falls upon landing will lose a full point.**

**The Soviet Union won the women's team gold medal at eight straight Olympics. Romania broke the streak in 1984.**

perfect 10s. But the perfect 10 hasn't disappeared entirely. It remains the best execution score a gymnast can receive. A gymnast who scores a 10 in execution has technically done a perfect routine. It is a rare and special thing.

McKayla was one of a few vaulters who have come close to scoring a 10 in execution. Her performance in the 2012 Olympic team final electrified her teammates. They performed the rest of their routines almost flawlessly. At the end of the competition, the United States had won its first Olympic team gold medal in 16 years.

Judges deduct points from gymnasts' scores when they make errors in their routines.

# 7

# INCREDIBLE
# KOHEI UCHIMURA

When he was just 15, Kohei Uchimura left his family in Nagasaki, Japan. He moved to Tokyo to receive better gymnastics coaching. Kohei knew he had a chance to be a great gymnast if he devoted himself fully to his sport. He wanted to become one of the world's best.

Kohei's first major competition was the 2008 Olympic Games in Beijing. He won a silver medal in the all-around. In 2009 Kohei became the world all-around champion for the first time. He repeated as world champion in 2010 and 2011, then won Olympic gold in the all-around in 2012.

Kohei Uchimura performs on the pommel horse at the 2008 Olympic Games.

## VITALY SCHERBO

**Vitaly Scherbo of Belarus starred at the 1992 Olympic Games. He won six gold medals, the most ever by a gymnast. He competed with athletes from other former Soviet states. They were called the Unified Team. Scherbo was the Olympic champion with his team, in the all-around, and in four individual events.**

That was only the beginning. Kohei repeated as world champion in 2013, 2014, and 2015. And he won his second Olympic gold medal in 2016. His six world titles is a record.

As a team, Japan won the all-around gold medal in five straight Olympics, from 1960 through 1976. The great Mitsuo Tsukahara and others performed moves that had never been done in competition. Japan faltered in the 1980s and 1990s. But Kohei helped put Japan back on top. In 2015 Japan won the World team gold medal for the first time in 37 years. And Japan followed that success with a team gold medal at the 2016 Olympics.

**Kohei shows his form in the six events that make up the men's all-around competition at the 2016 Olympics in Rio de Janeiro.**

# 8

# SUPERSTAR SIMONE BILES

By a quirk of fate, Simone Biles comes from a town called Spring, Texas. The US superstar shows terrific "spring" in her tumbling and vaulting. Biles is so powerful and flies so high that she astonishes even her coaches.

Biles discovered gymnastics by accident. When she was six years old, her daycare had scheduled a field trip to a local farm. The trip was cancelled, so the kids went to a gym instead. Simone was excited by what she saw. She began imitating the gymnasts, flipping and cartwheeling. Simone had

Simone Biles gets plenty of air on her tumbling passes.

Biles is a whirling blur on the vault.

never been in a gymnastics class. But she was able to do skills that normally take months or years to learn.

Simone's energy and talent were apparent to the gym's coaches. They sent her home with a note that asked her parents to send her back soon. Simone's parents were intrigued by the idea. Gymnastics could be a way to channel Simone's boundless energy. They enrolled her in classes.

Simone took to gymnastics immediately. But winning was never her main goal. Having fun and entertaining her teammates was more important to her than training for the Olympics.

In 2013 Simone turned 16. She was old enough to compete at the World Championships. Talented but untested, she surprised everyone by winning the all-around title. The United States had a new star gymnast.

## SIGNATURE SKILL

Biles's best event is floor exercise. She wows fans and judges by soaring to great heights on her tumbling passes. Biles even has an original tumbling skill named after her. She was the first woman to perform two straight flips with a half twist at the end. Gymnasts who invent moves often have the move named after them. So this special skill is now called "The Biles."

And she never looked back. Simone successfully defended her world title in 2014 and 2015. That made her the first female gymnast to win three straight world titles. She won

> **Biles edged her teammate Aly Raisman for the all-around gold medal at the 2016 Olympics.**

four gold medals at the 2015 World Championships. That brought her World Championships medal count to 10 in all. No other woman in history had won that many.

She sealed her place in history at the 2016 Olympics. She won the gold medal in the all-around, vault, and floor exercise. She also led the United States to a team gold medal. And she added a bronze medal on the balance beam.

Despite all that success, Biles remained focused on enjoying gymnastics. "What sets me apart is . . . how much joy I find in it," she said. "I have fun doing what I do."

Biles and teammate Aly Raisman smile for the cameras at the 2016 Olympics.

# 9

# TRAMPOLINE

Charlotte Drury had a dream. She hoped to compete at the Olympic Games with her best friends, Kyla Ross and McKayla Maroney. The three often talked about what it would be like to win a gold medal.

By the time they were 13, Kyla and McKayla had become elite gymnasts. But training was harder for Charlotte. One day she couldn't take it anymore. Charlotte decided to quit artistic gymnastics. But her days as a gymnast weren't over. She found a new type of gymnastics: trampoline.

Trampolinists soar higher than any other type of gymnast.

The trampoline provides plenty of spring to send the gymnasts airborne.

Most gymnasts use trampolines while learning or mastering new skills. But trampoline is a sport in itself. Trampoline gymnasts are also known as trampolinists. They perform combinations of flips in their routines while bouncing up to 30 feet (10 m) in the air.

A trampoline routine consists of 10 elements, all flips. Trampolinists must keep going during their routines.

Once they stop or bounce off the trampoline, the routine is over. They also try to land all their flips in the middle of the trampoline to avoid deductions from the judges. The more time a gymnast spends in the air, the better his or her score.

The Olympic dream came true for Charlotte's best friends. Kyla and McKayla made the US team for the 2012 London Games. They each won a gold medal as part of the US women's team. Charlotte has become one of the nation's best trampoline gymnasts. Trampoline became an Olympic sport in 2000. Injuries kept Charlotte out of the 2016 Olympics. But she hopes to make Team USA in 2020.

## THE LOST SPORT

Today it's a part of trampoline gymnastics. But tumbling also had a brief run as an Olympic sport. Tumbling was contested as a gymnastics event at the 1932 Olympic Games in Los Angeles. The gold medalist was American Rowland Wolfe. Wolfe was ahead of his time. Many of the tumbling elements he performed in 1932 were so difficult that gymnasts did not begin performing them on floor exercise until more than 30 years later.

# 10 RHYTHMIC GYMNASTICS

When Laura Zeng tells people she's a gymnast, they often picture the balance beam or the uneven bars. But Laura is not an artistic gymnast. From a young age, Laura has performed rhythmic gymnastics.

Rhythmic gymnasts' routines involve the use of artistic props. They include a hoop, a ball, a pair of clubs, and a long satin ribbon attached to a stick.

Rhythmic routines contain lots of leaps, turns, and dance steps. Routines are very expressive and often tell a story. But the gymnasts must keep

Laura Zeng performs with a ribbon at the 2015 Pan Am Games.

the props in motion. Rhythmic gymnasts toss and catch each item. Dropping or losing control of a prop can result in deductions from the judges.

Teams of five gymnasts perform in rhythmic group gymnastics. Each gymnast in the group has her own prop. But she often exchanges it with her teammates. Group routines are complex. Sometimes a gymnast will throw her prop into the air and then catch someone else's prop.

Rhythmic gymnastics was developed in eastern Europe during the early 1900s. It was popular in the former Soviet Union. Many of the best ballerinas also came from the Soviet Union. Ballet is closely linked with rhythmic gymnastics. Today the best rhythmic gymnasts often come from

## OTHER FORMS

Artistic, rhythmic, and trampoline gymnastics are the most well-known forms of the sport. But other types are also popular. Aerobic gymnastics features fast-paced music, aerobic steps, and dance. In acrobatic gymnastics, partners or groups work together to create dramatic and beautiful routines. And Gymnastics for All has something for everyone.

Rhythmic gymnasts use props in their routines.

Russia and other eastern European countries. One is Russian Yana Kudryavtseva. She has won three consecutive world titles in the sport.

Laura Zeng began by doing Chinese folk dance and ballet. But a friend introduced her to rhythmic gymnastics. She switched at age seven. In 2014, when she was just 14 years old, she represented the United States at the Youth Olympic Games. It was her biggest competition up to that point. She won an individual bronze medal.

# ALL ARE WELCOME

Oksana Chusovitina never wanted to stop doing gymnastics. Today she is one of the most famous gymnasts in the world. But not because she has the most gold medals. She's famous for a unique record that she holds.

Oksana was born in Uzbekistan in 1975. She began gymnastics when she was just a little girl. Her talent was obvious. She joined the national team of the Soviet Union. Oksana won two gold medals at her first World Championships in 1991. She also won a gold medal in the team competition at the 1992 Olympic Games.

At age 41, Oksana Chusovitina competed in the 2016 Olympics.

As Chusovitina got older, her teammates began to retire from gymnastics. They became coaches and judges. Chusovitina kept competing. By the time she was in her mid-20s, she was one of the world's oldest elite gymnasts. Chusovitina didn't care. She enjoyed gymnastics and continued to do well.

In 2001 Chusovitina's young son, Alisher, was diagnosed with leukemia, a dangerous form of cancer. Alisher could not be treated in Uzbekistan. The Chusovitina family went to Germany to find doctors who could help the little boy. Within a few years, Alisher was cured.

Chusovitina was grateful that German doctors cured her son.

## JUST A NUMBER

The world's best gymnasts are usually in their late teens or early 20s. But in recent years, older gymnasts have shown that they are still competitive. At the 2012 Olympic Games in London, Great Britain's Beth Tweddle was the oldest female gymnast to win a medal. She won bronze on the uneven bars. Tweddle was 27 years old at the time.

Chusovitina kisses her silver medal at the 2008 Olympics in Beijing.

She wanted to show the country her appreciation. So she decided to join the German national team. In 2008 Chusovitina won the Olympic silver medal in vault for her new country. She was 33 years old. That was already considered old for an elite gymnast. But Chusovitina still didn't feel ready to retire.

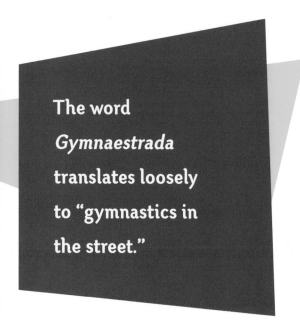

The word *Gymnaestrada* translates loosely to "gymnastics in the street."

At age 41 Chusovitina qualified for the 2016 Olympic Games in Rio de Janeiro, Brazil. She represented her home country, Uzbekistan. The Rio Olympics were her seventh consecutive Olympic appearance. No gymnast had ever done that.

Not everyone can go to the Olympics at age 41. Most elite gymnasts are younger than 20. But being older doesn't mean you can't be a gymnast. In fact, there is a gathering that allows gymnasts of all ages to show off their skills.

Gymnasts from around the globe celebrate the sport at the World Gymnaestrada.

The World Gymnaestrada began in 1953. It has been held every four years since. The World Gymnaestrada is a week-long event. Participants march in opening and closing ceremonies like in the Olympic Games.

German gymnasts perform at the 2015 World Gymnaestrada in Helsinki, Finland.

Gymnasts come from all over the world to show off their skills. Their routines are between three and five minutes long. They also make friends and celebrate the sport they love. All are welcome at the World Gymnaestrada.

All World Gymnaestrada participants perform at least three times during the week. Their performances showcase the best of all forms of gymnastics. The youngest participants are children. The oldest gymnasts tend to be in their 80s. It truly is gymnastics for all.

Not everyone gets to be an Olympic gymnast. But the World Gymnaestrada is an event for all who love gymnastics and want to participate. In gymnastics, everyone can find something they love to do.

The 2015 World Gymnaestrada drew more than 20,000 gymnasts from 53 countries.

# GLOSSARY

**all-around**
The main competition at a gymnastics event, in which gymnasts perform all events, with the highest combined score winning.

**elite**
The highest level.

**execution**
The completion of a task.

**giant**
A 360-degree swing around a bar.

**iron cross**
A strength position on still rings in which the gymnast hangs with his arms out to the side, the body forming the shape of a cross.

**release move**
A type of skill on uneven bars or high bar in which a gymnast lets go of the bar, performs flips or twists, and grabs the bar again without touching the ground.

**springboard**
A bouncy surface that gymnasts use to launch themselves into the air when vaulting or mounting the uneven bars or balance beam.

**tumbling pass**
A series of connected acrobatic skills that begins in one corner of the floor exercise and ends in the opposite corner.

# FOR MORE INFORMATION

## Books

Douglas, Gabrielle, and Michelle Burford. *Grace, Gold and Glory: My Leap of Faith.* Grand Rapids, MI: Zondervan, 2012.

Kawa, Katie. *The Science of Gymnastics*. New York: PowerKids Press, 2016.

Meyers, Dvora. *The End of the Perfect 10*. New York: Touchstone, 2016.

## Websites

To learn more about gymnastics, visit **booklinks.abdopublishing.com**. These links are routinely monitored and updated to provide the most current information available.

# INDEX

# ABOUT THE AUTHOR

Blythe Lawrence fell in love with gymnastics at the age of eight while watching the 1992 Olympic Games in Barcelona, Spain. She has written about gymnastics for Universal Sports, espnW, the *Seattle Times*, and Examiner.com. She dedicates this book to Glen, her childhood gymnastics coach.